Killer Tea Cosies

AND HOW TO MAKE THEM

Killer Tea Cosies

AND HOW TO MAKE THEM

The Watermark Press

First published in 1996
Killer tea cosies and how to make them was produced by
The Watermark Press
Sydney, Australia

National Library of Australia
Cataloguing in Publication data

Wallis, Annette
Killer tea cosies and how to make them
ISBN 0 949284 25 4

1. Tea cosies. 2. Knitting-Patterns. 3. Crocheting- Patterns
4. Sewing- Patterns. I. Wallis, Diane. II. Title.

Printed in Hong Kong

Acknowledgements

It is one thing to have an idea but quite another to turn it into a finished book. For producing Killer Tea Cosies, most of the credit must go to Nick Godlee, a costumier of extraordinary talents who made *Smiley, Jiggler, Planktonia, Diva, Belle, Cyberpot, Floribunda, Little Ben, Serpentia* and *Spike*. Diane Wallis made *Gladys* and *Hooty Hooty* based on a design from 'You Can Crochet' by Sharon White, reproduced with kind permission of Kangaroo Press. Annette Wallis made *Noelle* and *Tracey*. Sophie Blackall made the very regal *Regina* and also *Cat-a-Jekyll & Hyde-a-Cat*. Marina Hookham made *Henny Penny* and Melissa Bowman made *United Potions* and *Bugsy*. Where would we have been without their brilliance. The background photography for *Noelle* was generously supplied by Telstra Corporation and for *United Potions* by Aussat. All other photography is by Simon Blackall. The lighthearted introductory text is a distillation of prose and, dare we say it, poetry by Leith Hillard, Jenny Cattell and Simon Blackall.

Cosies Nostra

Bugsy

In the great melting pot of downtown Manhattan, lapsang souchong mixed in with Peppermint might well be NYC (Not Your Cup of tea). The blare of horns and the hustling crowds in the concrete canyons can overwhelm the visitor. But what do we see here, nudging its way through the traffic? A German double agent in secret silver service. Don't mess with this guy, he knows his Fortnum & Mason from his Smith & Wesson and he's not averse to taking a pot shot if the blend isn't right.

INSTRUCTIONS

MATERIALS

35cm green cotton drill

70cm white cotton drill

35cm fine cotton lining fabric

35cm wadding; scraps of grey cotton drill for car detailing

2.75cm black cord

piece of clear plastic, approximately 25 x 20cm

black embroidery thread

dressmaker's tracing paper and tracing wheel

4 appropriately shaped beads for headlights and brake lights

NOTE: Finish the ends of the cord either by singeing
or by applying a dab of craft glue.

TO MAKE THE BASIC CAR

■ Enlarge pattern so it measures 1.5cm larger all round than one side of your teapot.

■ Using the pattern, cut out two pieces of lining material, two pieces of wadding, four pieces of white cotton drill, and two pieces of green cotton drill. Mark and clip notches through all layers for alignment when assembling. A 1.5cm seam allowance is included.

■ Trace all design and quilting lines marked on pattern onto right side of green fabric using tracing paper and a wheel. Go over these lightly in pencil. Leaving an 0.5cm seam allowance to turn under, cut away front and rear windows from green fabric. Clip into curves of windows and turn back and press seam allowance. Tack in place.

■ Layer the green car front over one white cotton drill piece, matching notches, and mark steering wheel position on white fabric. Remove the green car front from the white piece. Using the black cord double, shape the steering wheel into the position marked on the white drill and then hand sew into place.

■ Cut two pieces of clear plastic to fit behind front and rear window 'frames'. Pin in place. Place the green car front onto the white drill, matching alignment notches. Tack around the edge of the car to hold in place. Machine top stitch around window. Repeat this process with the car back so both sides are at the same stage.

■ Using patterns, trace the front and rear bumpers, the bonnet handle and the rear boot handle onto the grey fabric. Allow a 0.5cm seam allowance for turn back. Cut out, turn back seam allowance, tack and press. Pin bumpers and boot pull onto car, following design lines. Machine top stitch in place.

■ Cut two small rectangles of white fabric, allowing 0.5cm turn back, to make front and rear number plates. Turn under allowance and tack. Pin in place on front and back, then top stitch. In pencil, draw numbers onto number plates.

■ Hand sew cord around front and rear windows.

■ Layer together one piece of white drill, one piece of wadding, then the green car front. Pin the three layers together, then loosely tack through all the layers using a long vertical stitch in preparation for quilting. Repeat the layering and tacking with the green car back.

■ Machine around perimeter of car front and car back on marked line. Machine along all quilting lines, as marked on your pattern. Hand sew black cord onto front and back.

FILLING IN THE DETAILS

■ Cut a square of grey fabric 3.5 x 3.5cm for front bonnet handle. Fold two sides of the square to the centre, then fold in half lengthwise. Turn short ends under and hand sew down. Hand sew handle in place on car, squashing it outwards so it is raised a little.

■ On the back, mark the grill detail in pencil using the template as a guide. Hand sew large continuous vertical stitches with embroidery thread.

■ Embroider numbers on front and rear number plates.

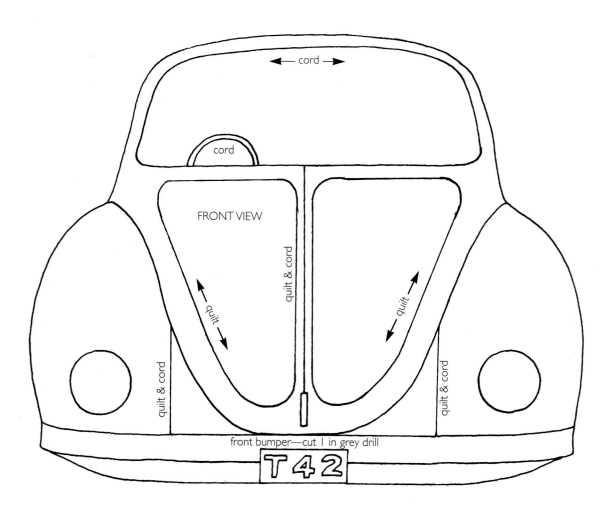

■ With right sides together, machine the front of the car to the back, leaving bottom open. Clip into curves and turn to right side. Sew two pieces of fine cotton lining together, leaving bottom open and a gap of approximately 15cm at the top.

■ With the right sides together and side seams matching, slip the lining over the car. Machine around bottom edge, joining the lining to the car. Pull car through opening in lining and turn lining to inside. Hand sew opening closed.

■ Using craft glue, stick the headlights and brake lights to the car.

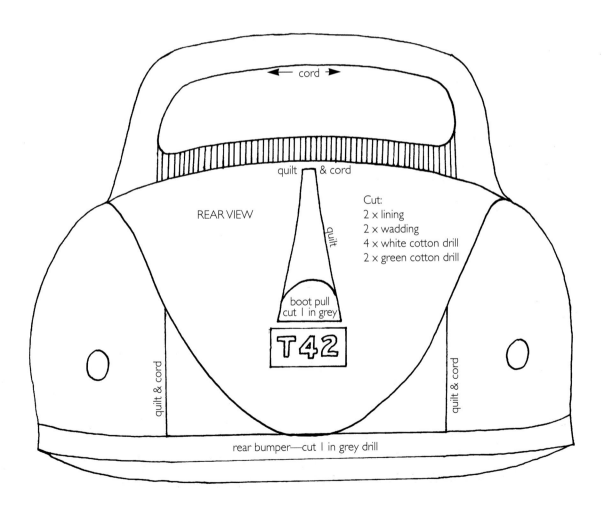

Floribunda

Show that special someone how much you care with an intoxicating gift of orange pekoe tips; such a fine bouquet. Floral tributes might be pleasing to some, but what could be more tender and touching than a burst of teapot cover artistry. Nature in all her most delicious and thirst quenching abundance brings a bloom to the cheek, a blossom to the smile, and a perennial overgrowth to the tea table.

INSTRUCTIONS

MATERIALS

13 x 70cm piece of coir matting

2m bias binding or cotton tape, 2.5cm wide

30cm each of lining and wadding

10cm white felt

20cm dark brown felt

10cm each of 2 shades of pink felt

10cm each of 2 shades of yellow felt

1 craft square in cream

10cm each of light green and medium green felt

20cm dark green felt

16 x 13mm pompoms, 8 yellow and 8 black

threads to tone

TO MAKE THE BASKET

■ Glue, or sew by hand, the binding onto the long edges of the coir matting. Turn the binding over the inside of the coir and glue or sew. Butt short ends of the coir together and glue binding over join and wrap to inside.

■ Cut out enough lining and wadding to fit around the inside of the coir basket and to line and pad underneath the oval-shaped top. Tack lining and wadding together and sew up with lining sides together. Slip inside basket and hand sew to binding at bottom of basket.

■ Cut out a brown felt oval for the top, about 10cm larger than the circumference of the basket. To raise the brown felt as a base for the flowers, place a lump of wadding underneath. Gather around the edge, then glue felt to bias binding inside the top of the basket.

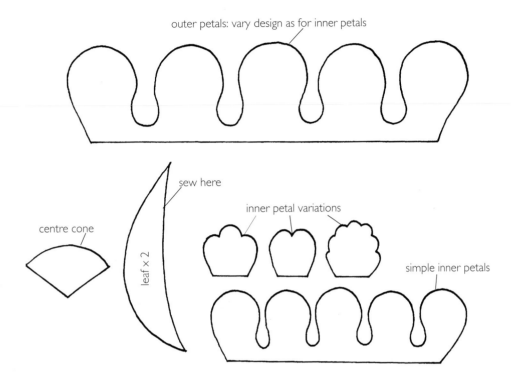

TO MAKE THE FLOWERS AND LEAVES

■ From the coloured felt, cut out strips of five petals joined at the base (see illustration), one set larger (for the outer petal) and in one colour tone, the other smaller (for the inner petal) and in a different colour tone. Gather up each strip around the base with running stitch. Place smaller petal strips inside larger ones and secure with a stitch.

■ To make the centre of the flowers, cut eight brown and eight white cone shapes. Wrap one cone shape around each pompom. Sew up seam and push needle through the pompom to catch it inside. Sew cone inside flower.

■ Cut half-leaf shapes from all shades of green and mix and match two shades together to form the leaves. Sew along the middle and press point flat.

■ Arrange flowers and leaves on the felt top and glue or sew down. Attach a novelty bee with wire for the finishing touch.

Cat-a-Jekyll & Hyde-a-Cat

Tea for two and two for tea
When you see him you don't see me
Which way will you pour?
Which cat will you see?
This two-faced feline warms the tea.

INSTRUCTIONS

MATERIALS

Felt, at least 60cm wide – 40cm white, 40cm orange, 20cm black

tracing wheel and coloured carbon paper

4 animal eyes; 1m wadding

40cm iron-on fusible web

thread – white, black, dark orange, pink

1m cotton lining; optional fabric paint – dark orange

TO MAKE THE CAT PATTERN

■ Enlarge pattern until it is 1.5cm larger all round than one side of your teapot – approximately 34cm high, 34cm wide, not including the tail. One side will be black and white, the other orange and white. With tail, the cat should measure 62cm wide, including 1.5cm seam allowances. Invent your own patches and features.

CUTTING OUT

■ Cut two cat shapes, without tail, from lining fabric. Allow for a 3cm hem along bottom edge. Cut two cat shapes, without tail, from wadding. Cut four cat shapes, with tail, from lining. Cut two cat shapes, with tail, from wadding. Cut one cat shape, with tail, from white felt. Cut one cat shape, with tail, from orange felt.

■ Sandwich tail-less linings between tail-less wadding, leaving allowed hem on lining to extend. Stitch around outside leaving bottom open. Fold up hem and whip stitch.

BLACK AND WHITE CAT

■ Take one lining with tail. Take white felt cat shape and mark details of features and patches with coloured carbon. Trace black patch shapes onto paper fusible web. Press onto black felt. Cut around patches, remove paper and iron in position onto white felt cat.

■ Tack white felt to lining. Close zigzag all feature lines (mouth in white and around all patches in black). Close zigzag nose and ear markings in pink.

■ Sandwich one tailed wadding between white cat shape and second tailed lining.

■ Quilt design lines and sew around outside edge.

ORANGE CAT

■ Make up as for the black and white cat, but reverse the pattern. The large zigzag pattern, as seen in the photo, may be painted with dark orange fabric paint. Close zigzag nose, mouth and ears in dark orange thread.

TO FINISH OFF

■ Bring right sides of the appliquéd cat shapes together and tack. Machine around the edge, leaving the bottom open. Sew up tail completely. Clip curves and corners. Turn up hem and sew. Turn right side out.

■ Put in eyes by making hole with a stitch ripper and pushing wire stems through.

■ Place tail-less cat shape (made up of the lining and wadding) inside the felt appliquéd cats. Hand sew in place along bottom edge.

■ With needle and thread, make one long stitch from nose to cheek for each whisker. Reinforce the stitches on the inside of the cosy.

ginger cat
left foot
cut × 1 white

ginger cat
right foot
cut × 1 white

left black and
white cat mask
cut × 1 black

right black &
white cat mask
cut × 1 black

cut × 1 black

cut × 1 black

ginger cheeks   cut × 1 white

Black and white cat
Reverse for ginger cat

Quilt and close zigzag all
interior design lines.
Appliqué and close zigzag all patches.

After enlarging, remember to add 1.5cm seam allowance to
edges of the cat-shaped pattern and to both sides of the join

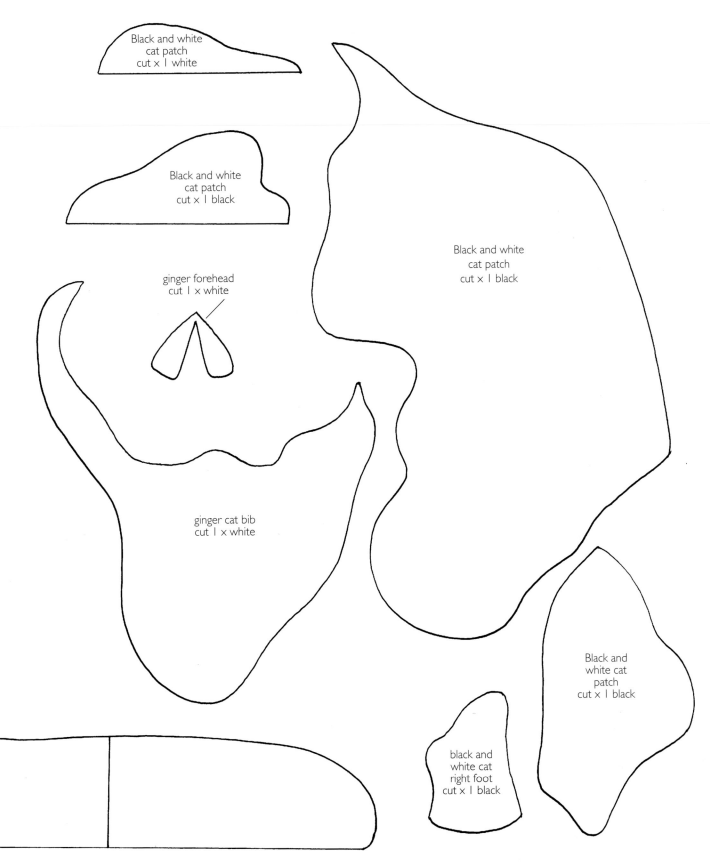

Black and white
cat patch
cut x 1 white

Black and white
cat patch
cut x 1 black

ginger forehead
cut 1 x white

Black and white
cat patch
cut x 1 black

ginger cat bib
cut 1 x white

Black and
white cat
patch
cut x 1 black

black and
white cat
right foot
cut x 1 black

Gladys

Up above the world so high, like a teapot in the sky. But can it be true? Is this a cuppa we see before us? Out, out of this glorious spout. And tea's the thing with which to catch the taste buds of a king.

INSTRUCTIONS

This simple rib cosy, made to fit a large pot, is extravagantly trimmed with crocheted pansies and leaves. The pattern uses 12-ply yarn for the cosy and 5-ply for the trim, but could easily be adapted for other yarns. Tapestry yarn is quite suitable for the flowers and allows a wide choice of colours.

MATERIALS

12-ply yarn (50g balls)
2 balls of black for basic cosy
scraps of 5-ply yarn in orange for tie
green for leaves
orange, black or other dark colour
white and various colours for pansies
5mm knitting needles
3.5mm crochet hook

TO MAKE THE SIDE (make 2)

■ Using 5mm needles and 12-ply yarn, cast on 41 sts. ■ Row 1. K1, *K1, P1; rep from * to last 2 sts, K2. ■ Row 2. K1, *P1, K1; rep from * to end. ■ Rep last 2 rows 20 times then Row 1 once OR until length desired, ending with Row 1. ■ Next row. K1, P2tog 20 times. ■ Next row. K1, *yfwd, K2tog; rep from * to end. ■ Next row. Purl. ■ Cast off.

TO MAKE THE TIE

■ Using 3.5mm hook and 5-ply yarn, make a length of ch about 60cm. ■ Work 1dc in each ch to end. ■ Fasten off. ■ For a thicker tie, work a second row of dc.

PANSY (Make about 20)

■ Using 3.5mm hook and orange yarn, make 3ch and join with a sl st to form a ring. ■ 2ch, 8dc in ring, sl st in 2nd ch at beg. ■ Fasten off.

■ Join dark yarn to same place as sl st, 1dc in same place as join, 2htr in next dc, 1dc in next dc, 3htr in next dc, 1dc in next dc, 2htr in next dc, 1dc, sl st in next dc. ■ Fasten off.

■ Join white yarn to same place as dark yarn join, 1dc in dc, *2tr in each of next 2 sts, 1dc in each of next 2 sts; rep from * once, 2tr in each of next 2 sts, 1dc in sl st, sl st in same place as last dark st. ■ Fasten off.

■ Join coloured yarn to first white st, 1dc in same place as join, 1dc in each of next 5 sts, *1tr in same place as dark dc below, 1dc in each of next 6 white sts; rep from * once, 1dc in same place as end of white, 1tr, 3dtr, 1tr in next orange st, 1dc, 1tr, 3dtr, 1tr in next orange st. 1dc in same place as beg of white, sl st in first coloured st at beg. ■ Fasten off.

LEAF (make about 20)

■ Using 3.5mm hook and green yarn, make 11ch. ■ Miss 1ch, sl st in each of next 2ch, 1dc in next ch, 1htr in next ch, 1tr in each of next 5ch, 8tr in last ch, working along other side of chain, 1tr in each of next 5ch, 1htr in next ch, 1dc in next ch sl st in each of next 2ch. ■ Fasten off.

TO MAKE UP

■ Join sides, leaving space for handle and spout. Thread tie through holes and tie in a bow. Place cosy on pot, then pin pansies in place while rib is stretched. Stitch pansies and leaves in position.

Regina

More pomp and a little less circumstance will provide greater warmth to regal tea parties. And so, beneath this ermine-trimmed, opulently bejewelled cosy sits the royal pot. A queenly brew enough for two. Take tea with The Queen and cup it sweet. But eschew the pot at her writing desk lest desk pot turn into a despot! Oh no!

INSTRUCTIONS

MATERIALS

30cm wadding; 30cm lining (pink satin or other)

50cm crimson velvet; 80cm gold fabric

10cm fake fur (white with black flecks. If you can only find white fake fur,

you will also need black feathers or black fabric paint)

3m stiff waistbanding 4-5cm wide

1m stiff waistbanding, 7-9cm wide

jewels, pearls, gold trim, as desired

craft glue; thread

Tip: When cutting artificial fur, cut from the underside, snipping carefully at the fabric and pulling fur fibres apart gently as you go. This will give you a more natural edge than if you cut directly through the fur from above.

THE BASIC CROWN

■ Measure your teapot – both height and circumference. Draw a semicircle the height of your teapot+2cm. The bottom edge (the diameter) should equal half the measurement right around the teapot (including handle and spout) +2cm.

■ Using this pattern and adding turn-up to bottom edge. cut two pieces from lining. Join, right sides together, leaving bottom open.

■ Using semicircle pattern cut two pieces from wadding.

■ Pin wadding to outer (wrong) sides of lining. Whip stitch all together, leaving bottom edge open.

■ Drape velvet loosely over the pattern shape. (It helps if you actually place your wadding/lining semicircle over your teapot at this stage to give it some shape.) Pin velvet loosely in gathers and fold the excess length around the bottom edge neatly. Fold up lining edge and turn in cut edge (as for binding or a hem). Sew lining hem to velvet, pleating or gathering velvet as necessary. Catch gathers and folds over top and sides of velvet with needle and thread. Remove pins.

■ Sit the cosy over your teapot again, and pin a length of waist-banding at left-hand seam edge. Take this strip up to top centre and, leaving a generous amount of slack, pin again. Repeat over to right bottom seam.

■ Cut at right bottom edge (after pinning). This is your 'long strip'.

■ Find centre-front and centre-back and repeat with leftover waist-banding, pinning at top with same amount of slack etc. Cut at bottom. This is your short strip. Once you have determined the length of the long and short strips, mark positions (centre-front and back etc) and remove.

■ Pin long strip to gold fabric. Leaving 1.5cm seam allowance at either side, cut two pieces. Repeat for short strip. Leaving waistband-ing pinned to fabric, sew down either side of two strips, taking care not to catch the waistbanding with the machine stitches. Remove pins and waistbanding.

■ Turn strips inside out and thread waistbanding through respective sleeves (strips). Finish ends. Pin long strip in position from side seam to side seam, short strip from front to back. Find centre of each strip, determine where they tran-sect and align this point with cen-tre-top of cosy. Catch strips to the velvet here at four corners.

DECORATING THE CROWN

■ Using the cross pattern opposite, cut two pieces from gold fabric. Sew around edges leaving bottom half of circle open, and turn inside out. Stuff with wadding scraps. Decorate with trim if desired. Cut disc of cardboard from circular part of cross pattern (minus seams). Place open base of cross over disc. Gather edges underneath and tack in place. Sew gold button or bead to centre of cross at either side. Attach cross to centre of strips at top of cosy. Arrange jewels and pearls along strips, glue in place and stitch if necessary when dry.

■ To make wide gold band (base of crown) measure circumference around the outside of cosy. Cut strip of wide waistbanding to this measurement. Pin to gold fabric, as before. Cut two pieces, plus seam allowance. Leaving waistbanding in place, sew down either side. Remove waistbanding and turn inside out. Insert waistbanding.

■ Turn in edges of gold fabric. Feed one end into the other and neatly whip stitch to join up band.

THE FINISHING TOUCHES

■ Cut fur trim (10cm wide) to length of band.

NOTE: If you have white fur, insert black feathers at intervals in the same direction, placing a dab of craft glue at the ends before parting fur and sticking in place. You could also paint black streaks on white fur with fabric paint.

■ Place right side of fur against right side of gold band (outer side) with lower edges matching. Sew fur to gold band. When you reach the seam, continue to sew short ends of fur strip together. Turn fur back the right way, then up and under to the inside of the band. Stitch along inside. (You may need to turn band inside out to make this easier.) Turn back the right way.

■ Sew pearl trim (or gold trim) around the top edge of gold band. Place velvet cosy inside gold band. Tuck in strips and catch in place at front and back, left and right. Catch in several places along top and bottom of gold band (attaching it to velvet cosy).

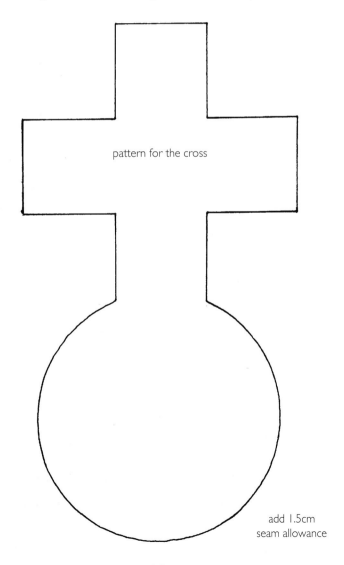

pattern for the cross

add 1.5cm
seam allowance

Hooty Hooty

The Owl was waiting at the waterside for
   the arrival of his dear,
He'd filled the pot and the tea was hot
   but ms pussy did not appear.
The Owl looked up to the stars above
   and gave a hoot and a moan,
And he said, where's the cup,
That cat's stood me up
I'll have to take tea on my own, my own,
   my o o own....
I'll have to take tea on my own.

INSTRUCTIONS

This pattern is ideal for scraps of knitting yarn. The amounts given in the materials list relate to the minimum quantity in which yarns can be bought. In some cases, only a fraction of the yarn will be used.

The first round for the eyes is worked with white and fawn mohair (using two strands) with the outer round in grey fluffy acrylic and fawn mohair. The bottom three rows of the body are worked in a combination of dark grey mohair and grey acrylic, moving up to fawn mohair and grey acrylic for the upper body. The 'outline' of alternate double crochet and chain is worked in a very dark navy blue.

The owl beak is actually a bear nose (available at craft supply shops) with a triangular piece of black felt glued on top. For the lining, although any 'owly' shade of between light fawn and black could be used, we chose a kind of donkey brown.

MATERIALS

5.00mm hook

5.50mm hook

100g grey fluffy acrylic

50g white 7-ply mohair

50g fawn 7-ply mohair

50g grey 7-ply mohair

50g navy 8-ply pure wool

50g brown 8-ply pure wool

4 owl eyes

2 owl beaks (bear noses glued with triangles of black felt)

MEASUREMENTS

■ This cosy will fit most 4-cup teapots.

TENSION

■ 15tr and 8 rows to 10cm over tr fabric using 5.50mm hook and 1 strand of 8-ply wool (for the inside lining).

TO MAKE THE EYE PIECE

■ Using 5.50mm hook and white and fawn mohair together, work 4ch, 1sl st back into the 1st of the 4ch to form a ring. ■ Row 1: 4ch, (this is equivalent to 1tr, 1ch); (1tr into ring, 1ch) 11 times; 1sl st in top of 3rd ch (12tr and 12 1ch spaces.) ■ Row 2: Change to grey acrylic and fawn mohair, 1sl st in 1st 1ch sp, 3ch, 1tr in same sp, (1ch, 2tr in next sp) 3 times, 2tr in each 1ch sp to end, 1sl st in top of 3rd ch. (12 groups of 2tr and 3 1ch spaces). ■ Fasten off.

Tip: Bobble means [yarn over hook, hook into sp, yarn over hook and draw yarn up to a height of 2cm (3/4")] 3 times, yarn over hook and draw through all 7 loops on hook, 1ch to fasten.

BODY (make 2)

■ You need two eye pieces. Use 5.50mm hook and fawn mohair and grey acrylic together.

■ Row 1: With front of first eye piece facing you, join yarn to 1st 1ch sp, 3ch, (bobble, 1 ch, bobble) in same sp, (1 ch, bobble, 1ch, bobble in next 1ch sp) twice; pick up second eye piece; with front of second eye piece facing you, work (1ch, bobble, 1 ch, bobble) in each of the 3 1ch spaces, 1tr in last 1ch sp beside bobble. (12 bobbles, 11 1ch spaces and 1tr at each end.) Turn.

■ Row 2: 3ch, (bobble into top of next bobble under 2 threads, 1ch) 11 times, bobble in last bobble, 1tr in top of 3rd ch (12 bobbles, 11 1ch spaces and 1tr at each end); turn.

■ Repeat Row 2 a further 6 times, changing to grey acrylic and grey mohair for the last 3 rows. ■ Fasten off.

NAVY STRIPE BETWEEN EYES (make 2)

■ Using 5.50mm hook and 2 strands of navy 8 ply wool, join yarn to middle of eye pieces (in second tr above body through both sides of the eye pieces together), work 1ch, 1dc in each of next 5tr.
■ Fasten off.

■ Attach eyes and beak. Darn in all ends.

INSIDE LINING (make 2)

■ Using 1 strand of brown wool only and 5.50mm hook, work 37ch.
■ Row 1: miss 3ch, 1tr in each ch to end (35tr). Turn. ■ Row 2: (1dc, 1ch) in 1st tr, 1tr in each tr to end (don't forget – last tr goes in top of turning ch). Turn. ■ Repeat Row 2 four times (35tr).

TIP: Dec means decrease: (yarn over hook, hook into next tr, yarn over hook and draw through, yarn over hook and draw through 2 threads only) twice; yarn over hook and draw through the remaining 3 loops. The decrease is worked over 2 trebles.

■ Row 7: (1dc, 1ch) in 1st tr, dec, 1tr in each tr to last 3tr; dec, 1tr in top of turning ch. (33tr). Turn. ■ Repeat Row 7 twice. (29tr) ■ Row 10: (1dc, 1ch) in 1st tr, 1tr in next tr, * dec, 1tr in next tr *; rep from * to * to the end (20tr). ■ Row 11: (1dc, 1ch) in 1st tr, dec, 1tr in each tr to last 3tr, dec, 1tr in top of turning ch. (18tr). ■ Row 12: same as Row 11. (16tr). ■ Row 13: (1dc, 1ch) in 1st tr, 1tr in each tr to end. (16tr). ■ Row 14: same as Row 13. ■ Fasten off. Darn in all loose ends.

NAVY EDGING

Side 1:

■ Pin body to inside lining with wrong sides together. With front side of body facing, using 5.00mm hook and 1 strand of navy 8 ply wool, join yarn to body just below eye piece (through both sides together).

■ Round 1: 1ch, 1dc evenly along side edge (through both sides together), 3dc in corner, 33dc evenly along bottom edge (through both sides together), 3dc in corner, 1dc evenly along side edge and around the head (through both sides together); 1sl st in 1st dc of Round 1. ***

■ Round 2: 1ch, 1dc in each dc along side edge, 3dc in corner dc, 1dc in each dc along bottom edge, 3dc in corner dc, 1dc in each dc along side edge finishing just below eye piece (do not work around head section).

■ Fasten off.

Side 2

■ Same as for Side 1 to end of Round 1. ***

■ Round 2: 1ch, 1dc in each dc along side edge, in corner dc work (2dc, 1sl st in corner of Side 1, 1dc), 1dc in each dc along bottom edge, in corner dc work (1dc 1sl st in corner of Side 1 2dc), 1dc in each dc along side edge, finishing just below eye piece; holding Side 1 and Side 2 together, 1dc in each dc around head section (through both sides together), 1sl st in 1st dc of Round 2.

■ Fasten off. Darn in all loose threads.

■ If desired, brush gently with a mohair brush for a realistic look.

Spike

Animal, vegetable, mineral, tea cosy? The
curious hedgecosy, bright of plastic eye,
hibernates between meals, reappearing only
on hearing the sound of the biscuit tin being
opened. He is partial to a fragrant brew (plenty
of milk please) and although shy, he is not in
the least bit prickly and will accept a nicely
buttered scone or crunchy cookie from
someone he barely knows.

INSTRUCTIONS

MATERIALS

1m maroon hessian

30cm maroon felt; 20cm cream felt

scrap of pink felt; scrap of brown felt

30cm lining; 30cm wadding

1 pair 1cm eyes; 1 bear nose

thread—cream, maroon

THE QUILLS

■ These are made with hessian fringing. Cut selvedge (3cm each side of material) off hessian. Make small clip every 5cm up one trimmed edge. Pull thread at each interval. Zigzag (set at widest zigzag) along one side of each 5cm section, cut into strips along pulled thread line. Fray trim down to zigzagging.

THE BODY

■ Enlarge the patterns to a size to fit your teapot. Cut out two identical pieces of maroon felt to form a dome shape large enough to cover your teapot generously. Mark where the fringing is to go. Mark on both pieces, with tacking, where the face will be attached.

■ Using zigzag stitch, sew fringing trim on each half, starting from tail end and placing edge of trim at marked lines. At about halfway, sew both body halves together, matching carefully. Press seam open. Sew on remaining trim over the centre seam line.

THE FACE

■ From cream felt cut two of face and one gusset. Mark the position for eyebrows and mouth. Cut them out of brown felt and sew them on. Attach the eyes. Make a small inner ear out of the pink felt and a larger outer ear out of the cream felt. Sew the pink ear onto the cream outer ear. Join face pieces from forehead to nose, then stitch gusset in place.

■ Sew on nose, turn face right way out and press under 1cm on all edges except the bottom. Stitch ears in place. Pin face to body (not at bottom edge) and slip stitch on. Stuff face lightly with wadding scraps.

TO FINISH

■ Cut out lining and wadding, the same shape as the hedgehog body but 2cm smaller all round. Sew wadding pieces to lining pieces around edge. Sew together with lining sides together. Slip inside body, turn 1.5cm hem of body inside and over wadding insert and hand stitch through all the layers.

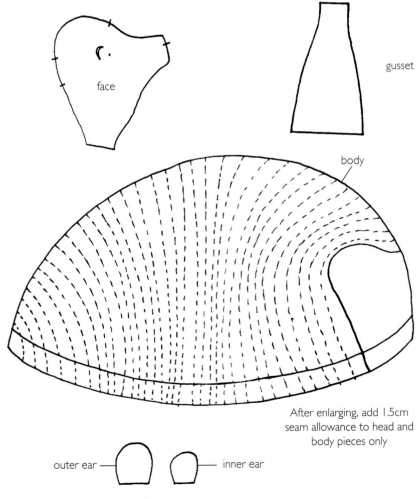

face

gusset

body

After enlarging, add 1.5cm
seam allowance to head and
body pieces only

outer ear — — inner ear

Planktonia

Posing on the rocks in some Scandinavian harbour, the seductive siren has sung the same song, luring lonely sailors to who knows what? Her mesmerising harmonies, rhythmically tuned to the human heartbeat, promise the fulfilment of secret desires: 'I've just put the kettle on. Come over for a nice cuppa and a little lie down.' Beware! Be warned! There's something fishy about this sexpot. One sip of her piping hot brew and you will be out of your depth.

INSTRUCTIONS

MATERIALS

40cm gold fabric; 20cm blue fabric
40cm calico; 20cm grey felt; 40cm grey fabric for back of cosy
20cm white felt for mermaid body; 1m lining
10cm scrap of dark green satin
thread — pink, grey, gold, light green, white
gold-painted shell; iron-on fusible web
beads for eyes; sequins in shades of blue and green

TO MAKE THE BASIC COSY

■ Enlarge the pattern so that two pieces when joined will fit your teapot. Allow room to spare for padding.

■ Using your pattern, cut out the cosy shape; one piece from calico, two pieces from lining, two pieces from wadding and one piece from grey fabric for the back of the cosy. Cut out gold fabric (for the hair) to fit the top three-quarters of the front and cut out blue fabric (for the sea) to fit the bottom quarter. Glue or sew the gold and the blue fabric to the calico to form the base for your picture.

TO MAKE THE MERMAID AND SEASCAPE

■ Draw shapes of grey rocks onto web paper. Cut out roughly and attach to grey felt with a hot iron. Cut out, peel off paper and iron on over join of blue sea and gold hair. Draw body of mermaid onto the web paper in the same manner. Cut out roughly and fuse to white felt with a hot iron. Then cut out white felt, peel off paper and press lightly into place onto gold and blue fabric.

■ Again using the web paper, cut out a tail in dark green satin. Apply to the front of the cosy and arrange the body on top, pressing firmly with an iron to adhere. Using the pink thread, zigzag around body and to define the body details.

■ Tack the whole of the front of the cosy to wadding and quilt around body shape and top of tail to give a raised effect. Tack wadding to back of cosy and sew the back of the cosy to the front. Sew lining pieces together, leaving a gap to turn through at the top. Sew lining to cosy around lower edge and turn through the small gap. Sew up opening by hand.

TO FINISH THE COSY

■ Sew on sequins, starting with dark green, then light green, dark blue, then light blue, gradually changing the tone. Make the eyes by sewing a bead inside a sequin.

■ Using a light green thread, zigzag details onto the green satin tail.

■ Cut wave heads out of white felt and glue on. Straight stitch around to secure.

■ Sew gold shell on the top of the cosy.

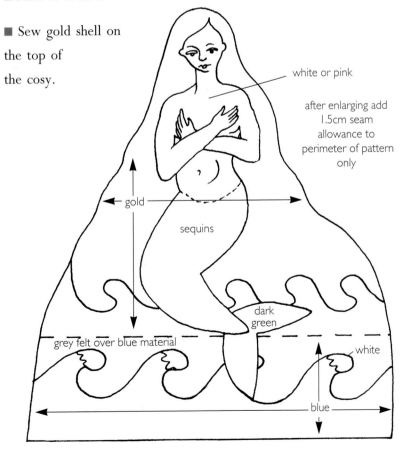

Diva

This spectacular cosy brings a world-class performance to the tea table — and high drama to your taste buds as you sip your first cup of tea from this operatic pot. Our prima donna, known for her tempestuous brew, warbles a high C as the scalding tea simmers beneath her generous frame. La Giganta, as the cognoscenti call her, will always give you a steaming cuppa, a bit of vibrato and a good time — she knows the score.

INSTRUCTIONS

MATERIALS

dressmaker's carbon paper; tracing wheel

10cm blue felt; 40cm beige felt; 10cm black felt; 70cm white felt

60cm calico; 60cm lining

1.3m narrow black trim

1.5m thick wadding

thread — white, black, beige, blue

TO BEGIN

■ Enlarge pattern pieces to twice the size shown here (200% on photocopier) and then add 1.5cm seam allowance to all outer edges. Mark design lines on right side of your pattern with tracing wheel and coloured marking paper.

TO MAKE THE BASE

■ Cut out the felt pieces using the pattern and trace the coloured marks onto the right-hand side. Starting with white felt pieces and working down to blue, stitch down each marked coloured edge. Tack each body part onto wadding and sew up body with right sides together: sew a dart up the back; sew in front and sew in back.

TO MAKE THE SHELL ROOF

■ Tack wadding to outer pieces of all shells and sew up the spine (curved seam). Sew inside to outside with right sides together, leaving opening between the two notches. Turn the right way and press edges a bit flatter. Sew up gap by hand.

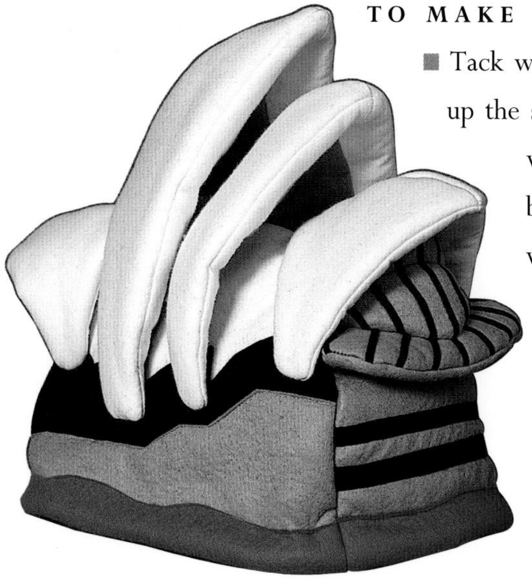

TO MAKE THE WINDOW

■ Sew trim along marked parallel lines. Tack to wadding.

■ Sew matching pieces with right sides together around edge from notch to notch. Turn through and hand sew gap. Quilt a horizontal line on the upper window.

■ Hand catch bottom of upper window to line on lower window, matching lines. Catch top of window to line inside shell no 1. Sew shells to body at three points as marked. Turn a 1.5cm hem, tack up by hand.

■ Sew lining, as for body, and sew in to body with a 1.5cm hem pressed up.

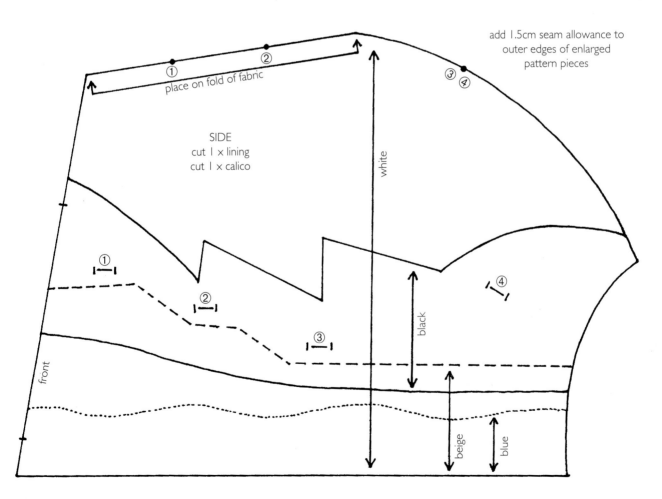

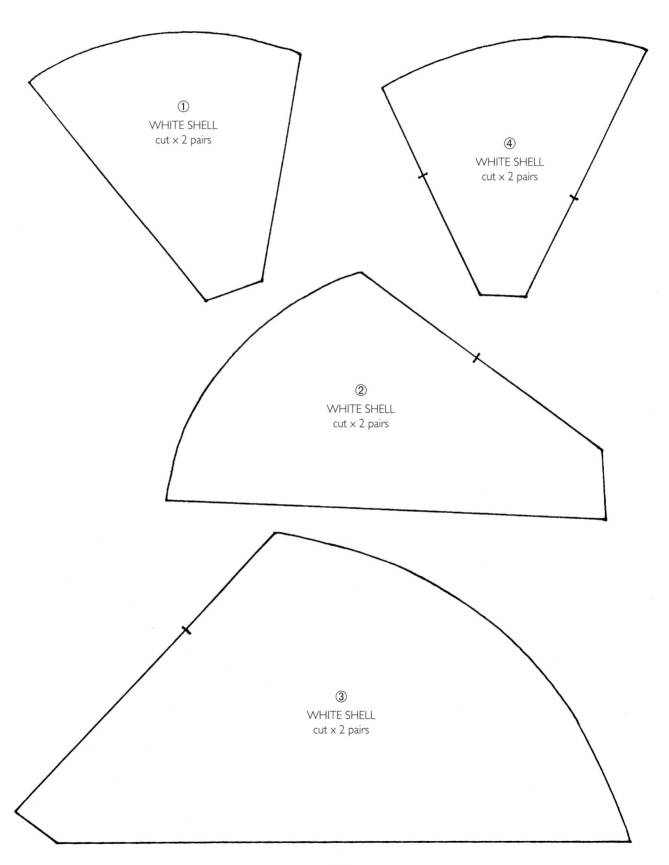

① WHITE SHELL
cut × 2 pairs

④ WHITE SHELL
cut × 2 pairs

② WHITE SHELL
cut × 2 pairs

③ WHITE SHELL
cut × 2 pairs

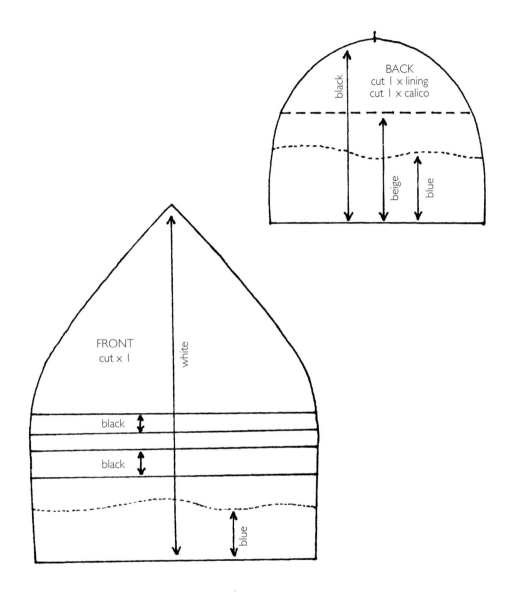

BACK
cut 1 x lining
cut 1 x calico

black

beige

blue

FRONT
cut x 1

white

black

black

blue

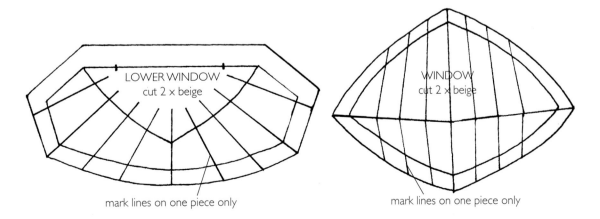

LOWER WINDOW
cut 2 x beige

mark lines on one piece only

WINDOW
cut 2 x beige

mark lines on one piece only

Noelle

Adoration of the crocheted cosy, anyone?
Hooked on puddings? Need something a little
festive for your hot pot? Noelle will oblige.
Although she is spirited, this lady's not for
boiling, burning or cutting thank you. And nor
will you choke on her charms; they are all
firmly attached with strong thread. Keep your
tapers and hot brandy for the real thing and
leave this rich little dish to her pot.

INSTRUCTIONS

■ This cosy is made in two pieces. The pudding, which is the basic cosy shape, is begun in the cream yarn, or scrap of any colour, to eliminate the need for a second ball of brown yarn. The Brandy Sauce top has chain drips of varying lengths and is stitched in place on the pudding, then decorated with a sprig of holly. Use a purchased holly decoration, or make your own from felt, fusible interfacing and red beads.

MATERIALS

1 ball of cream 8-ply yarn (50g ball)

1 ball of varigated brown 8-ply yarn (50g ball)

4mm crochet hook

pudding charms

holly decorations or materials to make your own

BRANDY SAUCE TOP

■ Using a 4mm hook and cream yarn, make 3ch and join with sl st to form ring. ■ Rnd 1: 3ch, 11tr in ring, sl st in 3rd ch at beg...12tr counting 3ch as 1tr. ■ Rnd. 2: 3ch, 1tr in same place as sl st, 2tr in each tr around, sl st in 3rd ch at beg...24tr. ■ Rnd 3: 3ch, 1tr in same place as sl st, *1tr in next tr, 2tr in next tr; rep from * 4 times, 1tr in next tr, sl st in 3rd ch at beg...36tr. ■ Rnd 4: 3ch, 1tr in same place as sl st, *1tr in each of next 2tr, 2tr in next tr; rep from * 4 times, 1tr in each of next 2tr, sl st in 3rd ch at beg...48tr. ■ Rnd 5: 3ch, 1tr in same place as sl st, *1tr in each of next 3tr, 2tr in next tr; rep from * 4 times, 1tr in each of next 3tr, sl st in 3rd ch at beg...60tr. ■ Rnd 6: *1dc in next tr, 5ch, miss 1ch, sl st in each of next 4ch, 1dc in same place as last dc, 1dc in each of next 4tr; rep from * around varying lengths of the chains for the drips from 3ch to 7ch at random, sl st in first dc. ■ Fasten off.

PUDDING

Using cream yarn, work first 5 rnds as for Brandy Sauce Top.
■ Change to variegated brown yarn. ■ Rnd 6: 3ch, 1tr in same place
as sl st, *1tr in each of next 4tr, 2tr in next tr; rep from * 4 times,
1tr in each of next 4tr, sl st in 3rd ch at beg...66tr. ■ Divide for
openings, Row 1: 3ch, 1tr in each of next 32tr, turn. ■ Rep Row 1
five times. ■ Fasten off. ■ Join yarn to next tr on Rnd 6 and work
Row 1 seven times in all. ■ Cont in tr across 6th row of first side, sl
st in 3rd ch at beg of 7th row of second side...66tr. ■ Next Rnd:
3ch, 1tr in each tr around, sl st in 3rd ch at beg. ■ Rep last rnd
once. ■ Fasten off.

TO MAKE UP

■ Stitch Brandy Sauce top to centre of pudding, catching down chain
drips. Stitch charms to pudding and holly to centre of frosting.

TO MAKE HOLLY

■ Fuse green felt to heavy fusible interfacing, and cut out four holly
leaf shapes. Stitch leaves to top with some red beads in the centre.

Belle

Waiting to gain the confidence of some courteous Southerner, our soft hand-sewn carpet bag is on the threshold of gracious living. Will she succumb to the blandishments of some halitosic hustler? Will Rhett ride back to scoop her up for a quick Darjeeling? If 'frankly you don't give a damn' then this could be the cosy for you. The pliant pot pours comfort for Southerners. But don't expect something for nothing.

INSTRUCTIONS

MATERIALS

100 x 70cm piece of carpet (very thin so it's easy to sew)

or a 60cm piece of patterned velvet

40cm lining; 31 x 43cm wadding

46 x 12cm (at least) of leather or vinyl

2 pieces of timber, 1.5 x 28cm

thread to match lining

handle ends, buckles, handbag latch

black paint; gold paint or gold marker

THE BASIC BAG

■ Cut out carpet rectangle 56 x 31cm and fold in half across its length; the fold will be the site for the wooden 'frame' and handle. Enlarge pattern to twice the size shown opposite (200% on photo-copier) and cut two carpet side sections. Turn over the top of side sections 1.5cm and top stitch. Sew to main bag section.

■ From inside, staple or nail the timber to fix it to the top of bag.

■ Cut out one 31 x 43cm piece of lining and one of wadding. Tack together near edges. Fold in half lengthways, sew up sides and press up lower edge 1.5cm.

TO FINISH OFF

■ Make up straps, punch holes and put in buckles. Make handle with a strip of leather with ends folded underneath, and long sides sewn down. Cut label and paint, or write with ballpoint pen, the letters T. E. A. Paint a thin gold line along one edge of the wood and mark gold dots 2cm apart on both sides. Sew straps onto edge, 6cm from side seams, and glue to wood, 6cm from each end.

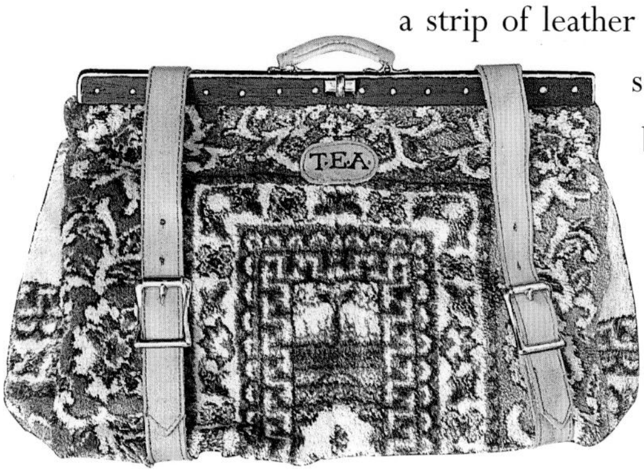

■ Put handle ends on and fix handle to them with wire. Glue on fake fastening.

■ Slip lining and wadding inside and hand sew in.

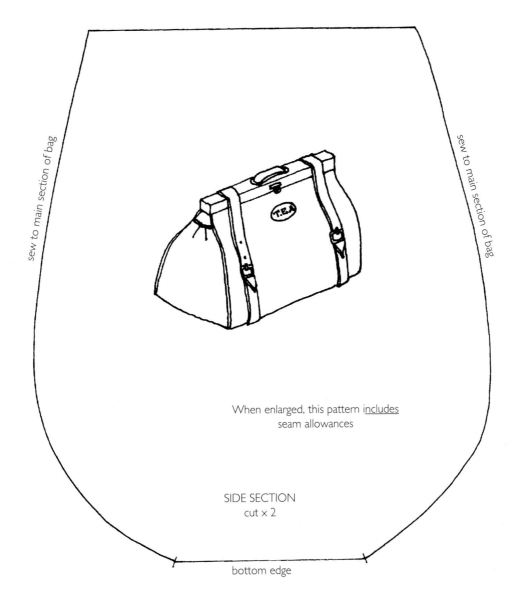

sew to main section of bag

sew to main section of bag

When enlarged, this pattern includes seam allowances

SIDE SECTION
cut x 2

bottom edge

United Potions

Look to the skies, you earthlings. You are not alone in the galaxy. Only now is the full story revealed of the Tea Thousand and One Space Odyssey, the United Potions that blasted off from Cup Canaveral into the black vastness of space. Waltzing sedately through the cosmos to the strains of the Blue Danube, they take their tea the milky way. It's the galactic way to global tea warming.

INSTRUCTIONS

MATERIALS

60cm white cotton drill

30cm white lining fabric

30cm wadding

3.25m gold braid

1.28m gold fringing (fringing used double for density)

12 national flags (15 x 7.5cm)

TO MAKE THE COSY

■ Enlarge the pattern to make a basic square, about 30 x 30cm, with room for six flags. Using the pattern shape, cut out four pieces of white cotton drill, two of wadding, two of lining.

■ Allow a gap of 12cm in the centre of the left side of the pattern for the handle, and 8.5cm in the centre of the right side of the pattern for the spout. Mark notches at the top and bottom of the gaps to ensure they can be matched.

■ Arrange the flags on two of the pieces of white cotton drill. Tack in place and then machine around each flag.

■ Layer together 1 of the flag pieces, 1 of the wadding pieces and 1 of the backing pieces (also white drill). Pin, and then machine, right around the edges, securing the 3 layers. Repeat the layering, pinning and machining with the remaining flag piece, wadding and backing piece.

■ With right sides together and notches matching, pin around the perimeter, leaving bottom open and a gap between the notches. Machine stitch pieces together.

FINISHING OFF

■ Sew together lining in the same manner. Slip lining inside cosy, wrong sides together, making sure the holes for handle and spout match up. Slip stitch lining to cosy at spout and handle holes. Turn up hem on cosy and slip stitch the lining to it.

■ Hand sew gold braid onto cosy, highlighting each flag, the top and the sides.

■ Machine the two layers of gold fringing together, pin in place on cosy, then hand sew.

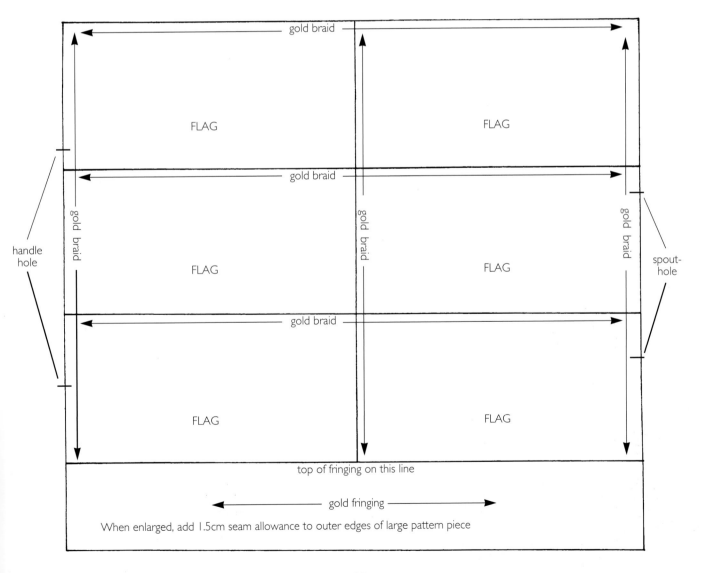

Cyberpot

The Silicon Valley cosy turns a nice cup of tea into an enhanced support system with optimizing characterization parameters; it facilitates downloading and delays job quitting by cleaning the mental screen and emptying the trash of the day. Time to shut down? No longer are you the server, but a chooser and teapot user. Select style options (milk, sugar?) and troubleshoot the breeze with friends, but beware; the jargon virus cancels out all possibility of meaningful interfacing.

INSTRUCTIONS

MATERIALS

20cm silver vinyl

20cm wadding

20cm lining

30cm very stiff interfacing

black thread

computer pieces

circuit boards from a junk shop

very strong glue

TO MAKE THE COSY

■ Make patterns for a kite-shaped top, 30cm long and 23cm wide along diagonals with two adjacent sides measuring 18cm and other two adjacent sides measuring 20cm, and 1 rectangle 77 x 19cm for sides. Cut one of each in interfacing, wadding, lining and silver vinyl.

■ With pencil, mark lines for stitching as shown opposite on both interfacings, extending and amending them as necessary. Tack interfacings to wrong sides of matching vinyl pieces.

■ Using black thread quilt, using marked lines as a guide.

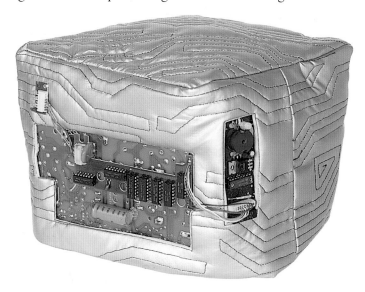

■ Choose your circuit boards and trace around each one on interfacing. Draw 5mm inside that line. Place on silver side of panel where desired and attach with small stitches. Cut out centre, leaving 1cm seam allowance; clip into corners, turn to inside, press. This makes the 'window' to accommodate your circuit board.

■ Join the two short ends of silver fabric. Sew in the top. Sew up lining with wadding (leaving part of top open). Turn inside out, place lining/wadding over vinyl assembly, right sides together, and stitch around bottom of cosy. Turn through the gap and stitch it closed by hand. Glue circuit boards inside the windows, against the interfacing, and add any other scraps of computer bits that are suitable.

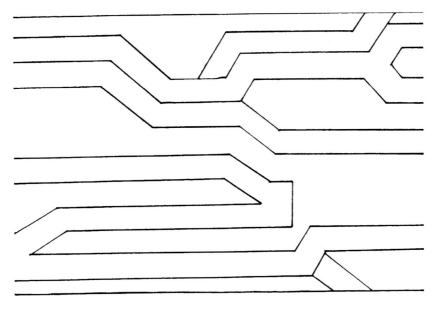

Henny Penny

Which came first: the chicken, the egg or the tea cosy? It's probably six of one and half a dozen of the others. Just as the humble egg is the genesis of all life, so does the cup of tea have life-giving properties for all those of broody disposition. Just as the cock crows, calling us, still dozy, into the dawn of another day, so the cosy enables us to face the world afresh with a comforting Breakfast Tea under our belts.

INSTRUCTIONS

MATERIALS

1m textured cream cotton fabric; 1m lining; 1m wadding; 70cm of 8cm-wide natural cotton fringing; scraps of red felt for wattle and comb and scraps of yellow cotton for beak; 2 small buttons for eyes or 2 small glass teddy eyes

TO MAKE THE BODY AND WINGS

■ Enlarge the pattern pieces to fit your teapot taking into account that the back panel inserted beneath the tail accounts for about one fifth of the circumference of the base. From textured cotton, cut out two body pieces, one underneath tail piece on fold, and one back panel for the hen's rear end — our back panel pattern was 16cm wide and 23cm high with an arched top to give breadth to the tail.

■ Cut one wadding and one lining for each of the two body pieces. Sandwich wadding between lining and textured cotton body pieces and baste around the edges. With right sides together, stitch around centre seam from lower front to tail end. Turn to right side. Cut out wadding and lining for back panel, layer as for body pieces and baste around edges.

■ Cut four textured cotton and two wadding wings. Place two cotton pieces together with one wadding on top. Sew around the edge leaving a gap, turn through the opening so wadding is inside the wing. Repeat for the other wing. Slip stitch openings closed and quilt wings to look like feathers. Hand sew the wings to the body.

TO MAKE THE TAIL

■ Stitch the textured tail underneath to the outside edge of the tail, right sides together. Turn to right side and quilt to form feathers. Sew back panel in place, straight edge at the base.

FINISHING OFF

■ Align top of fringing with base of cosy, overlapping ends. Machine stitch at edge and 3cm up from edge. Smooth fringe ends down over base. Cut two pieces of red felt for comb. Cut four pieces of red felt for the wattles. Cut two pieces of yellow cotton for beak. Sew together two pieces of comb, leaving a gap. Fill loosely with wadding scraps. Repeat for beak. Stitch beak and comb in place. Sew two pieces of wattle together and hand stitch to cheek. Repeat for other wattle. Sew on button or teddy bear eyes.

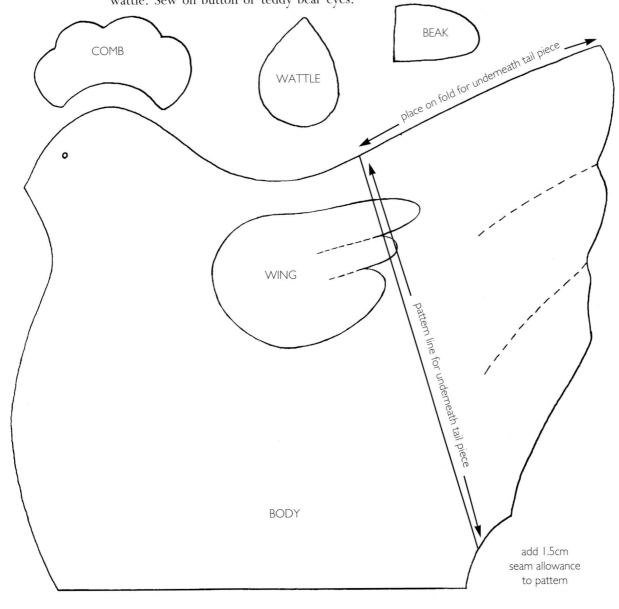

COMB

WATTLE

BEAK

place on fold for underneath tail piece

WING

pattern line for underneath tail piece

BODY

add 1.5cm
seam allowance
to pattern

Serpentia

Into Eden came Adam; from Adam's rib came Eve; from the serpent came the apple that tempted Eve to bite, (as well as the first pair of snakeskin boots with matching belt). On a blanket of greenery, Serpentia awaits to tempt you as she coils seductively round the pot. Meanwhile the kettle hisses softly and you succumb to the beady eye of our green friend. The tea draws. You take that first sip and are suddenly aware of your nakedness. Paradise is lost!

INSTRUCTIONS

MATERIALS

70cm light green felt; 40cm dark green felt
1 reel of green thread (in a shade between both green felts)
scrap of red felt, scrap of black felt
1m wadding; 1cm eyes

TO MAKE SNAKE BODY

■ Enlarge patterns to twice the size shown here (200% on a photo-copier). Cut light green felt into strips 16cm wide, with the head pattern on the end of one strip and the tail pattern on the end of another. On each strip, mark long diagonal criss-crossing lines, about 5cm apart – the stitching guide for the snakeskin pattern. Butt strips end to end and zigzag stitch the strips together to make a piece about 3.2m long.

■ For the bands on the snake, cut out 35 pieces in dark green felt, 16cm long with wavy edges. Pin the bands at slightly irregular inter-vals on the light green body, covering any joins, and sew down both sides to secure.

■ With green thread and guided by the marked diagonal lines sew a criss-cross pattern at intervals the width of the machine foot to make snakeskin pattern.

■ Sew up the dart in the tail and sew green lines across it at 1.5cm intervals. Sew fea-ture lines on the head and attach the eyes.

TO MAKE THE HEAD AND TAIL

■ Sew into mouth corners to reinforce; clip, and sew mouth darts. Starting at the head, join together 10cm of long seam. Press seam open.

■ From scrap of red felt, cut out the mouth. Cut tongue 11cm long and catch its straight end in the curved dart in the middle of mouth. With right sides together, sew mouth to head. Turn to right side.

■ Sew 10cm of tail end. Stuff head and tail with scraps of wadding. Cut remainder of wadding into 25cm strips. Butt ends of strips together and whip stitch together. Form into a long sausage, place inside snake and hand sew the seam closed. Press snake to flatten.

■ Coil the snake around your teapot, pinning into a shape that is easy to get off and on. Hand sew to secure.

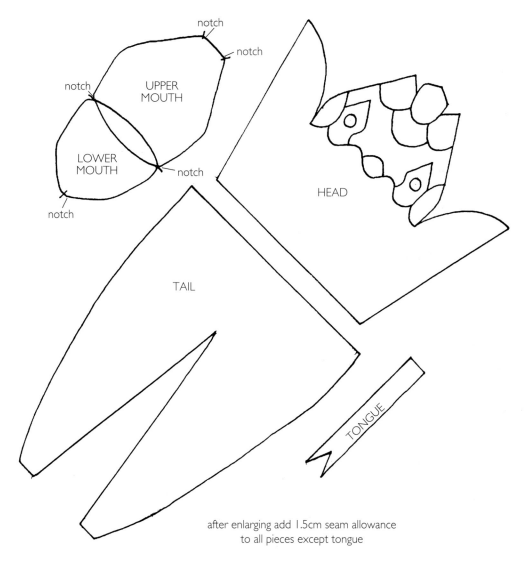

after enlarging add 1.5cm seam allowance
to all pieces except tongue

Smiley

During the War of Cold Tea, one pot came in from the cold. Head and shoulders, lid and handle above the crowd, stands this item that bravely attempts to bridge the gap between the cosy and teapot market. Grandly conceived and crafted from twinings of beaten gold, this ambitious cosy works best when used in conjunction with a most humble teapot.

INSTRUCTIONS

MATERIALS

30cm blue cotton fabric; 20cm cream chintz

2m gold trim

20cm gold fabric; 20cm black felt for negative area

iron-on fusible web

30cm of thick wadding

30cm black fabric for lining

gold ball for lid and elaborate gold accessories as desired

TO MAKE THE TEAPOT

■ Enlarge patterns to twice the size shown here (200% on a photo-copier). Cut out the body sections from the pattern. Smiley took six panels of blue fabric (with six of lining and six of wadding). Strips of cream chintz were used as a decorative feature around the base.

■ To allow for handle and spout, cut a front gap out of one body section and a back gap out of another body section. Do the same with the lining and wadding. Tack blue material to wadding, sew long seams to make up body, making sure the front and back gaps end up opposite each other.

■ Cut out lid panels in cream chintz and wadding (see pattern). Back each chintz panel with wadding and baste to anchor. Trim off. Sew lid sections on long sides, right sides together, stopping 1cm short of top.

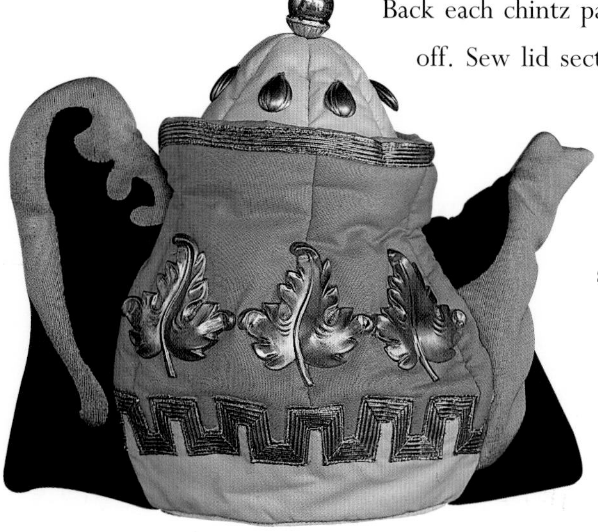

■ Cut out lower strip with turret pattern in cream and sew on gold trim. Top stitch strip in place. Sew on upper rim trim.

TO MAKE HANDLE AND SPOUT

■ Using pencil and paper and being gen-erous with fit and seam allowances, determine shape and size of sections covering handle and spout on your own teapot. Cut both of these shapes out of the gold fabric. Cut out the black negative shapes and place in pairs on web paper. Attach to black felt with hot iron, cut out, press in position to gold fabric. Pin to wadding, sew around edge and all around black to give quilted effect. With right sides together, sew spout and handle halves. Pin handle and spout to body of cosy, with right sides together, matching seam lines. Sew in lid, then catch down top edge of the blue section above the gold trim to form a rim.

■ Make up whole lining, minus lid, and with right sides together, sew to teapot along bottom edge. Turn through to right side. Press bottom edge so seamline is eased to the inside.

■ Sew ball to top of lid from the inside, pulling tight. Close gap at top of lining with a circle of fabric hand stitched into position. Finish decorating with gold ornaments as desired.

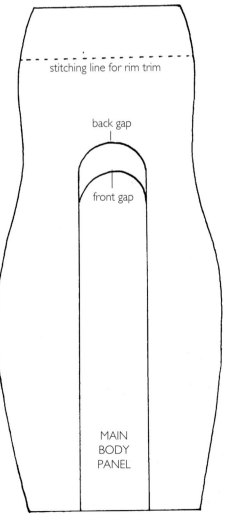

after enlarging, add 1.5cm seam allowance to patterns

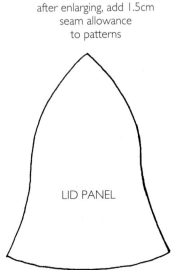

LID PANEL

MAIN BODY PANEL

Little Ben

Let's face it, you've got to hand it to a clock that always shows the same time. No matter when you look at it — it's always time for tea. It can be said that this little clock has the tea addicts' interests deep in its inner workings. No need to count the minutes until the next life-saving, heart-warming draught of sweet scalding brew. Time and tea wait for no one but relief is instant with this fellow.

INSTRUCTIONS

MATERIALS

70cm corduroy

70cm lining

70cm wadding

20cm white satin for face

1 metre of 3mm silver trim

black felt craft square

20cm iron-on fusible web

threads to match

TO MAKE THE PATTERN

■ Enlarge the pattern to fit the height and width of your pot. From corduroy, cut two identical clock shapes to make front and back of cosy. Mark on the details of the face and the back door and keyhole.

■ From the corduroy, cut a rectangular panel, 19cm wide, to join the two clock shapes.

TO MAKE THE FRONT

■ Reinforce corners at stitching line with short stitch and clip into corners. Reinforce 2mm outside dial hole and cut out dial hole 2mm inside stitching.

■ Cut two dials, one out of white satin and one out of interfacing. Mark centre, outside points and hour positions. Press interfacing onto back of satin dial.

■ Draw back-to-front numbers onto web paper. Press onto black felt, cut out and position on the dial with numbers 7mm from the edge. Position 1cm black felt lines for the minutes and two longer and wider felt pieces for the hands.

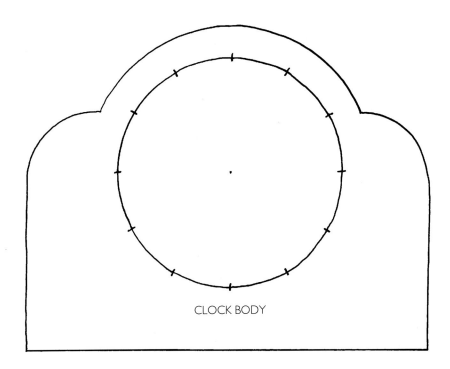

CLOCK BODY

Pin the clock face into position behind the hole on to clock front and then sew in place with a zigzag stitch. Sew two rows of silver trim around it, butting ends together and zigzagging across them.

TO MAKE THE BACK

■ Place interfacing behind where the door will be and zigzag satin stitch the door shape in black. Press on black felt keyhole shape and top stitch in place.

■ Taking the corduroy rectangle, sew 1.5cm down either long side. Clip along sides to 5cm from ends. Pin to front and back pieces and sew in place.

■ Cut out lining and wadding from the three clock pattern pieces. Sew together, as for the main body, leaving a small gap somewhere to turn through. Trim off 2cm at lower edge. This will ensure a neater finish. Sew lining to the base of the clock, right sides together. Turn through to right side.

HANDS

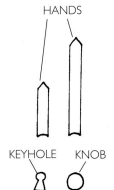

KEYHOLE   KNOB

Jiggler

The sharp-edged elegance of this creation confounds the tea connoisseur who raises a disdainful nose at the sight of this colossal swinging bag. A modern architectural creation of shimmering planes and vaulted ceilings that traps the blended leaves and reeks of all our tomorrows. But hark, beneath this modern frisson lurks a pot. Life is merely an illusion (or is it an infusion?) and reality pours forth.

INSTRUCTIONS

MATERIALS

70cm heavyweight non-woven interfacing; 40cm wadding
40cm white cotton fabric; 20cm brown felt
10cm red, 10cm yellow, 20cm green cotton fabric
30cm iron-on fusible web; 80cm piping cord (for string)
20cm wire (for staples)

TO MAKE THE BAG

■ Cut out interfacing and mark foldlines at one long edge, as shown.

■ Cut strip of the brown felt, 15 x 78cm and fuse to web with hot iron. Cut top edge in undulating shape. Cut leftovers into shapes like tea leaves. Fuse to straight edge of felt to one long edge of interfacing, leaving 1.5cm short at one end, and scatter tea leaf shapes close to the undulating line. With an iron, fuse them in place.

■ Fold and press creases as shown in the diagram, overlap long edge 1.5cm and top stitch.

■ To make the lining, cut two pieces of the white cotton in a dome shape large enough to cover your teapot, making sure each straight bottom edge is 42cm wide. Cut two pieces of wadding the same shape.

■ Tack white cotton pieces to wadding. Sew with cotton sides together on curved edge. Turn so the lining is outside.

■ Turn interfacing section inside out (felt outwards) and slip it over the lining with interfacing seam matching one lining seam. Pin and sew at 1.5cm. Fold top of interfacing, corners inward, then fold the top over.

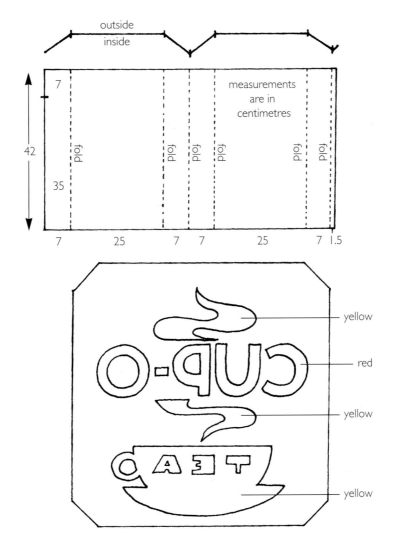

TO MAKE THE LABEL

For the label, which is 14cm square, draw a design onto fusible web paper in sections, according to colour. Fuse each colour section to the fabric, holding a hot iron on it for 15 seconds.

■ Cut out parts. Cut out label shape in interfacing. Press fabric label shape to interfacing shape. Arrange all parts on green label, as in the picture. Press on with hot iron for 15 seconds (do not allow iron to slip).

■ Make two wire staples, 6cm long, and fold. Punch holes in label and top of bag, and push through, catching string to inside of cosy, top of cosy and label.

Tracey

Sheltered beneath architecture of questionable provenance, our crocheted cosy confronts the unfinished Ionic column. Undaunted by the brazen pediment squatting defiantly atop the bold entablature and ignoring the sullen crepidoma at its base, she sighs wistfully over the lack of an ornamental triglyph. Behind her a sculpted urn, before her the Bay of Naples. The view stretches away to infinitea... Soon the tourists will return and slake their thirsts from her ample pot. *O sole mio,* she sings, as the sweet Darjeeling tips mash gently beneath her woollen skirts.

INSTRUCTIONS

The technique for making the bobbles on the green section of this tea cosy is different from the usual bobble method. The increasing is performed by 'making two' which is described in full in the abbreviations. Initially, this is a bit difficult. But after practice – it needs to be executed with the tips of the knitting needles – you will master the technique and revel in its beauty and efficiency. When decreasing from the bobble, by performing this with the purl-five-together method described here instead of just literally purling five stitches together, you get a very neat 'stalk' section between each leafy bobble.

MEASUREMENTS

■ To fit 4 to 6 cup pot measuring between 15 and 18cm high.

MATERIALS

12-ply wool (50g) 2 balls green

8-ply wool or acrylic (25g) 1 ball each of lilac and purple

and a small quantity of pink

1 pair 5mm knitting needles

a cable needle

3.5mm crochet hook

wool needle for sewing up and embroidery

TENSION:

10 sts and 16 rows to 5cm over patt.

SIDE

■ Using 5mm needles and 12-ply wool cast on 37 sts. ■ Row 1: K1, *P2, K1; rep from * to end. ■ Row 2: K3, *P1, K2; rep from * to last st, K1. Rep rows 1 and 2 once more. ■ Row 5: K1, *P2, M2, K1, M2, P2, K1; rep from * to end...61 sts. ■ Row 6: K10, *P1, K9; rep from * to last st, K1. ■ Row 7: K1, * P2, K5, P2, K1; rep from * to, end. ■ Rep Rows 6 and 7 once more. ■ Row 10: K3,

*P5tog, K2, P1, K2; rep from * to last 8 sts, P5tog, K3...37 sts. ■ Row 11: K1, *P2, K1, P2, M2, K1, M2; rep from * 4 times, (P2, K1) twice...57 sts. ■ Row 12: K3, *P1, K9; rep from * 4 times, P1, K3. ■ Row 13: K1, * P2, K1, P2, K5; rep from * 4 times, (P2, K1) twice. ■ Rep Rows 12 and 13 once more. ■ Row 16: K3, *P1, K2, P5tog, K2; rep from * 4 times, P1, K3...37 sts. ■ Rep rows 5 to 16 incl twice more. ■ Work rows 1 and 2 twice then row 1 once. ■ Row 41: K1, *K2tog, P1; rep from * to last 3 sts, K2tog, K1...25 sts. ■ Row 42: K1, *P1, K1; rep from * to end. ■ Row 43: P2tog to last st, K1...13 sts. ■ Row 44: Knit. ■ Row 45: P2tog to last 3 sts, P3tog...6 sts.

■ Cut wool leaving 30cm, thread through rem sts on wool needle, draw up and fasten securely, leaving wool to join side seams.

■ Make another side the same.

CROCHETED FLOWERS

■ Using 3.5mm hook and 8-ply yarn, make 3ch and join with a sl st to form a ring. ■ Rnd 1: 1ch, 9dc in ring, sl st in first ch at beg...10dc, counting first ch as 1dc. ■ Rnd 2: 1ch, *5tr in next dc, 1dc in next dc; rep from * to last dc, 5dc in next dc, sl st in first ch at beg. ■ Fasten off.

■ Make 4 lilac flowers and 5 purple flowers.

TO MAKE UP

■ Join side seams for 8cm from top, leave a gap of 9cm for spout and handle then join the last 3cm. Using pink yarn, stitch on flowers with five lazy daisy stitches over Rnd 1, one purple flower at centre top and the other arranged equally around it.

ATTACHING THE FLOWERS WITH
LAZY DAISY STITCH

■ In traditional embroidery, lazy daisy stitch gives the impression of petals. Here, the detached chain stitch worked in a circle fixes the flowers to the tea cosy and also acts as a contrasting centre for all the flowers.

■ Begin with a double thread in a wool needle and make a double stitch to anchor the thread on the tea cosy at the centre point for the flower. Position the flower on the tea cosy and bring the needle up through its centre. Hold the thread with your thumb where it is coming out of the centre of the flower, put the needle in through the centre of the flower again and bring it out at the base of one of the five treble sections crocheted in round 2, loop thread under needle point and pull the needle through. Insert needle on the other side of the looped stitch and bring it out again in the centre.

■ Make five 'petals' in all, finishing with a double stitch on the wrong side of the tea cosy to fasten off.